The Arctic
and
Antarctica

Roof and Floor of the World

Alice Gilbreath

DP DILLON PRESS, INC.
Minneapolis, Minnesota 55415

Library of Congress Cataloging-in-Publication Data

   Gilbreath, Alice Thompson.
   The Arctic and Antarctica : roof and floor of the world /
by Alice Gilbreath.
     p.   cm. — (Ocean world library)
   Bibliography: p.
   Includes index.
   Summary: Describes various aspects of the Arctic and
Antarctica including the animals that live there, the people
who have explored them, and the changes brought to these
faraway regions by modern technology and the search for
new energy sources.
   ISBN 0-87518-373-5 : $11.95
    1. Polar regions—Juvenile literature. [1. Polar regions.]
   I. Title. II. Series.
G590.G55   1988
998—dc 19   87-32448
                                               CIP
                                               AC

Dillon Press, Inc., 242 Portland Avenue South
Minneapolis, Minnesota 55415

Printed in the United States of America
   4 5 6 7 8 9 10 97 96 95 94 93 92 91 90 89

To T'Alana,
Bryan, Daniel,
Laura, Michael,
and Sami Lynn

Acknowledgments

I am grateful to Wayne E. Smith, Lt. Col., USAF (retired) for checking this manuscript and for his helpful suggestions.

Photographic Acknowledgments

The photographs are reproduced through the courtesy of the Alaska Division of Tourism; Alaska News; *Department of the Navy, Office of Information (Robert Carlin, artist, and official U.S. Navy photographs by PH3 William R. Curtsinger, PH1 G.V. Graves, PH2 Carl H. Jackson, Sr., PH1 David B. Loveall, PH1 T. Milton Putnam, PH1 Paul L. Schlappich, PH2 J. Urciuoli, and PH1 Robert L. Ziesler); Jim Gasparini and Will Steger/Firth Photo Bank; National Archives; and Norwegian Information Service in the United States.*

Contents

 *Arctic and Antarctic Facts*

Physical Makeup:
>   *Arctic*—water surrounded by land
>   *Antarctic*—land surrounded by water (about 5,100,000 square miles, or 13,209,000 square kilometers)

Average Temperatures:
>   *Arctic*— -30°F (-34°C) in winter; 30°F (-1°C) in summer
>   *Antarctic*— -40° to -80°F (-40° to -62°C) in winter; 32°F (0°C) in summer

Native Animals:
>   *Arctic*—polar bear, caribou, reindeer, arctic fox, lemming, walrus, ringed seal
>   *Antarctic*—leopard seal, Weddell seal, Adélie penguin, Emperor penguin, red krill

Native Peoples:
>   *Arctic*—Inuit, Lapps, Zyrians, Evenks, Yakuts, Tungus, Nenets, Chukchis, Koryaks, Kamchadals
>   *Antarctic*—none

Location of the Poles:
>   *North Pole*—90° latitude north, in the Arctic
>   *South Pole*—90° latitude south, in Antarctica

Months of Constant Daylight:
    North Pole—March to September
    South Pole—September to March

Months of Constant Darkness:
    North Pole—September to March
    South Pole—March to September

First to Reach the North Pole:
    By dogsled—Dr. Frederick A. Cook (April 21, 1908) or
                      Admiral Robert E. Peary (April 6, 1909)
    By plane—Admiral Richard E. Byrd (May 9, 1926)
    By submarine—Commander William Anderson and
            crew of the *Nautilus* (August 3, 1958)

First North Pole Expedition (Dogsled) to Include a Woman:
Ann Bancroft, Steger International Polar Expedition
(May 1, 1986)

First to Reach the South Pole:
    By dogsled—Roald Amundsen (December 16, 1911)
    By plane—Admiral Richard E. Byrd (November 29,
        1929)

Strangely shaped ice formations rise from McGregor Glacier in Antarctica.

 **The Ends of the Earth**

Huge **glaciers*** thousands of feet deep, towering cliffs of moving ice, thundering **icebergs** the size of Connecticut—all form part of the rugged beauty and vast open spaces of the Arctic and Antarctica. The ends of the earth are places where extremes are normal, where for months at a time day and night never end. They are distant, hidden, changing places that have challenged and fascinated the people who have lived in or explored them.

Imagine what it would be like to travel to the top and bottom of the world—the **North Pole** and the **South Pole**. Early in the twentieth century, daring explorers, traveling by dogsled, first reached the Poles. Since then a number of other explorers have made similar journeys over the ice, and many others have traveled there by plane. In the 1950s a nuclear-powered submarine, the *Nautilus*, made the first undersea (and ice) trip to the North Pole. Today, the United States maintains the Amundsen-Scott South Pole re-

*Words in **bold type** are explained in the glossary at the end of this book.

search station, where nineteen people live year round.

The North and South Poles lie far within the most remote and least known regions on earth. Both the Arctic and Antarctica are extremely cold, ice-covered areas that test the survival skills of people and animals. Yet in many ways the "roof" and "floor" of the world are different.

Much of the Arctic is a moving, frozen ocean of sea ice, which borders the northernmost parts of Asia, Europe, and North America. Antarctica is a continent, covered in most places by an **ice cap** more than a mile (1.6 kilometers) deep, and surrounded by ocean waters and currents. In some places high mountains and valleys rise above the level of the immense ice cap. Parts of the Arctic change from sea ice to open ocean during the short arctic spring and summer. During this brief season, snow disappears from large areas of arctic land. Flowers bloom, insects and birds fill the sky, and animals roam among the ponds and lakes of the "arctic prairie." Almost all of Antarctica remains ice-covered throughout the year, although some of the ice does melt in the surrounding ocean. Sea mammals and birds in the sea and coastal areas are the only animals of any size that live in the antarctic region.

People have lived in the Arctic for thousands of years, and have adapted to the bitterly cold climate and long, dark winters. They settled mainly in the coastal areas, where they could fish and hunt seals and whales. Some groups settled inland, where they hunted wild caribou or herded reindeer. Wherever the arctic people lived, they made their clothes from animal skins and followed the rhythm of the seasons.

After the early explorers reached the North Pole, people from the "south" began to take more of an interest in the lands of the far north. During World War II, nations built military bases in the Arctic, and the region has since become an area vital to the forward defenses of the United States and the Soviet Union. In the 1960s and 1970s, the discovery of oil and the building of the Alaska pipeline brought thousands of workers to Alaska's North Slope. Valuable deposits of coal, iron, and other minerals have also been developed in areas throughout the Arctic. The newcomers and the modern ways they brought with them caused rapid changes in the lives of the native arctic peoples.

Until nations established modern research stations in Antarctica, no one lived there in a permanent settlement. Scientists followed, or accompanied, the

early explorers, and today Antarctica has become the site of a variety of important scientific research. As in the Arctic, oil and other minerals lie beneath the coastal waters and ice-covered land. Yet, because of cooperation among a group of nations with research stations there, Antarctica remains the last undeveloped and unspoiled continent on earth.

Why are people attracted to these faraway places where cold, wind, ice, and snow make life itself a constant challenge? For some, the chance to explore one of the world's last frontiers is reason enough to make such a long, difficult journey. For others, the opportunity to work or to conduct research in a remote, beautiful, and peaceful area of the world has a strong appeal. For everyone who travels to the Arctic and Antarctica, the experience is an adventure—for many the adventure of a lifetime.

A native Alaskan.

2 The Roof of the World

If you stood at the North Pole, deep within the vast region of arctic ice, you would be looking down from the top of the earth. From the North Pole, there is no north, east, or west. There is only south.

Several million square miles of water form the **Arctic Ocean**—the roof of the world. Here, the world's northernmost ocean borders the northern fringes of Alaska, Canada, Greenland, Norway, Sweden, Finland, and the Soviet Union. Much of the ocean's surface water is frozen in layers of sea ice.

Some of the arctic ice has remained frozen for centuries. As new ice forms under the old, the top layer heaves upward, cracking the surface. Huge chunks break off. These broken pieces of floating ice are called **ice floes**. They bang against each other and freeze together. After cracking and breaking and refreezing many times, ice floes are stacked in some places like hills. Such ice hills are filled with large caves and steep cliffs that make them difficult to cross.

This map of the Arctic shows the region with the North Pole at its center.

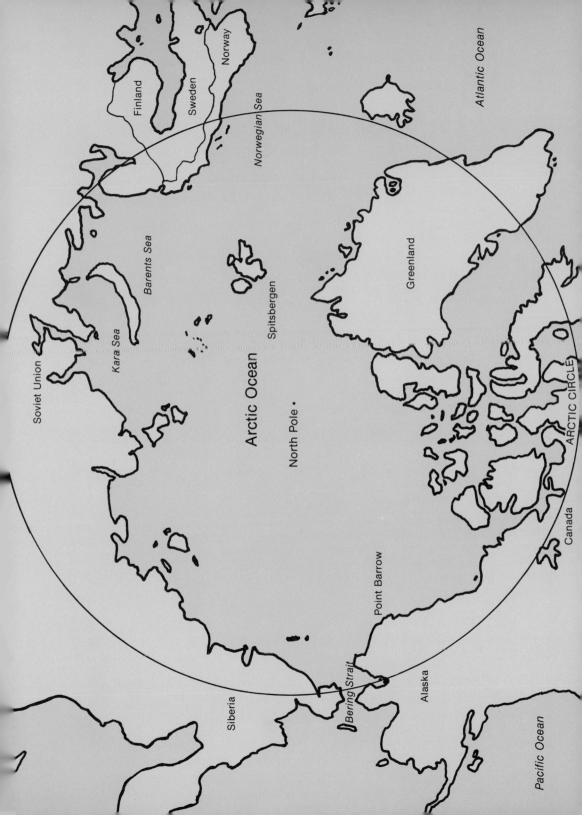

Finland

Sweden

Norway

Atlantic Ocean

Norwegian Sea

Barents Sea

Spitsbergen

Greenland

Kara Sea

Arctic Ocean

Soviet Union

North Pole ·

ARCTIC CIRCLE

Canada

Point Barrow

Siberia

Bering Strait

Alaska

Pacific Ocean

Ice floes in the Arctic Ocean.

    In the Arctic Ocean, currents of water flow beneath the ice. Most of these currents are cold. One, the **Gulf Stream**, carries warmer water from an area of the Atlantic Ocean far to the south.

    An ice cap is a very large mass of ice, called a glacier, which forms when snow packs so solidly that it becomes ice. Part of Greenland is covered by an ice cap thousands of feet deep.

Icebergs on the Move

Most arctic icebergs form at the edge of an ice cap. The weight of such an enormous glacier causes it to move slowly downward. When the glacier, moving a few inches each day, reaches the ocean, large pieces at the edge—icebergs—break off.

An iceberg, which is many times higher than a large ship, floats in the ocean because it is lighter than ocean water. Since icebergs are formed from fresh water—rain or snow—they do not contain salt. The lack of salt makes an iceberg lighter than the salty ocean water that supports its weight.

What we see of an iceberg is only a tiny part of it. Only about one-eighth of an iceberg extends above the water. The far larger, underwater part can cause great harm to ocean-going vessels. Icebergs have damaged and sunk many ships, including the *Titanic*, which sank in 1912. Icebergs such as the one hit by the *Titanic* may last for three years and melt when they drift south into the much warmer waters of the Gulf Stream.

Icebergs often form in the spring, when the arctic ice begins to melt. Then, ships can travel through parts of the Arctic Ocean. In September, this ocean again

Most icebergs break off from the edge of an ice cap, and they may float through the ocean for months or years.

begins to freeze. Soon tiny ice crystals cover the water. As they freeze into a solid sheet, fields of sea ice form at the surface. Below the surface, the ice becomes thicker and thicker. In one year, it may become eight or nine feet (2.4 to 2.7 meters) thick. Ice that does not completely melt during the summer months may form a rock-hard layer fifteen feet (4.6 meters) thick within a few years.

Arctic Weather—Day and Night

Throughout much of the year, the arctic region stays extremely cold. In some parts, temperatures drop to -80°F (-62°C). Yet, the temperatures alone do not provide an accurate picture of how severe this cold can become. Wind, combined with these low temperatures, creates conditions that threaten the lives of people who explore this vast area of ice and snow. Storms may come up suddenly. Dense fogs often reduce **visibility** to a few yards.

The **arctic whiteout** is another hazard for those who travel here. When clouds are thick in the sky and the ground is covered with snow, a traveler cannot tell where the sky stops and the snow begins. An object that appears to be close by may actually be miles away.

Because of the earth's **rotation**, or spin, the arctic ice moves all the time. Slowly, it drifts clockwise from Alaska and Siberia toward Greenland. And since the earth tilts to one side as it spins, the North Pole sometimes points toward the sun and sometimes away from it.

During the spring and the summer months, the Arctic tilts toward the sun. Then, at the exact top of the world, the sun never sets. For six months, it shines twenty-four hours a day. During the fall and winter months, when the North Pole tilts away from the sun, there are six months of darkness. In arctic areas to the south of the Pole, the periods of total daylight and darkness last for less than six months.

During the long arctic night, sometimes the sky brightens with flickering lights or a steady glow of bands of pale light. These moving light beams, tinged with red, yellow, green, or violet, are known as the **aurora borealis**, or northern lights.

Since part of the Arctic is frozen all year, people did not discover until this century that most of it is an ocean. Along the edges of the ocean, though, lies a huge area of treeless land that supports a great variety of animals and plants.

Spring and Summer in the Arctic

The white coat that the Arctic has worn all winter changes suddenly in the spring. Snow begins to disappear on the **tundra**—the land bordering the Arctic Ocean and reaching south to the edge of the northern forests.

The Tundra Comes Alive

The tundra, sometimes called the "arctic prairie," covers one-tenth of the earth's land surface. In the spring, after a very long winter, cracks appear in the ice at the edge of the ocean. The ice and snow of the tundra melt, leaving pools. Since **permafrost**, the permanently frozen subsoil beneath the pools, is as hard as rock, this melted water has no place to go.

Soon, mosses and **lichens**—tiny plants that are a combination of algae and fungi—begin to grow. The arctic sky fills with birds that **migrate** to the north from southern areas where they live during winter months. Geese, loons, swans, and plovers appear.

Some have come from as far away as Florida. The
arctic tern flies an incredible 11,000 miles (17,700 kilometers) from Antarctica to its arctic breeding grounds.
The birds jostle and fight as they search for food and
places to build nests.

Sparrow-sized snow buntings arrive after a 3,000-
mile (4,830-kilometer) journey. Males come first to
select nesting sites. Females arrive three weeks later.
The Arctic is an excellent place for buntings to nest
because they find an abundant supply of mosquitoes
to feed their young.

Eggs of mosquitoes and flies have been frozen all
winter. During the spring, these eggs hatch, and insects fill the air. Even though birds eat many of them,
the sky remains full of insects.

As the great thaw continues, the ice begins to
break apart. Huge pieces overturn and crash into the
sea. Ice floes break apart and drift away in open sea
lanes. As the weather grows warmer, more ice breaks
away from land, and storms blow it out to sea. Now, it
is easier to see where land ends and the ocean begins.

All plants and living creatures seem to be in a
hurry during the short arctic spring and summer. Very
rapidly, plants grow, flower, and bear fruit. Birds and

A flock of snow geese fills the sky over the arctic tundra of northern Alaska.

animals mate and raise their young. Many creatures shed their winter coats and acquire coats that blend with their summer surroundings. It is a time of plenty and a time of great activity.

On the tundra, the sun gradually comes up earlier and sets later until, by about the middle of May, it no longer sets. It circles the sky twenty-four hours each day. Offshore, thawing snow picks up the sun's warmth and a little water covers the ice. On land, snow slides down the slopes. Where the warmer temperatures of the tundra meet the colder temperatures of the ocean, fog forms.

The boggy tundra, almost free of snow, has a fresh carpet of grasses and reindeer moss. Now, too, the tundra blossoms with brightly colored plants. Purple saxifrage spread across the valleys. Arctic poppies cover plateaus. Buttercups fill the meadows. Even vegetable crops can be raised under the constant sunshine.

A foot or two below these blooms, the permafrost layer remains frozen. In some places, permafrost reaches down only a few feet. In other places, it reaches more than 1,000 feet (301 meters) beneath the surface.

Animals of the Tundra

Herds of migrating caribou graze along the foothills and paw away snow to reach tasty lichens. Packs of wolves follow, waiting for the chance to separate a single animal from the herd. Wolves will continue to hunt the caribou as long as they remain here.

Musk oxen also graze on the tundra. However,

A caribou with magnificent antlers moves along the foothills of a rugged area in Alaska.

they are not such easy prey for wolves. When threatened, the males form a tight circle around the females and calves, standing shoulder to shoulder, with their heads facing out. With their dark, shaggy coats and sharp horns, the bulls make an impressive, and effective, barrier. Wolves quickly learn to leave the musk oxen alone and look for easier meals.

Meanwhile, other animals are beginning to come out of **hibernation**. Arctic ground squirrels emerge from their burrows. They dig up rootlets to eat, along with sprouts and leaves. These creatures have survived the winter with an average body temperature of just 34°F (1°C) and only a few heartbeats per minute.

Lemmings, too, become restless. Some of them became meals when arctic foxes dug them out of their burrows during the winter months. The surviving lemmings seem to come out all at the same time and dart here and there until they cover the tundra. Owls and hawks snatch them for meals. Soon, their burrows will be flooded by streams of melting snow. Each female lemming has several litters of babies during the spring and summer. The babies have to grow rapidly to be able to live through the arctic winter.

As **pack ice** breaks up, polar bears come to land.

A group of polar bears rests on snow-covered ground in northern Alaska.

Their winter hunting is finished, and now they feed on lemmings or dead seals and whales that have been washed ashore. During the summer months, polar bears often have trouble getting rid of excess heat. They must cool off by lying on the ice or getting into the water.

Arctic foxes also come to land from the pack ice. On the tundra, they feed on birds, eggs, and lemmings.

As the weather grows warmer, their coats change to a brown-gray color that blends with their surroundings. When snow falls, their coats change back again to white. Then only a black nose and yellowish eyes keep them from blending completely with their winter territory.

As summer passes, the sun begins to dip below the **horizon**. Each day it sets a little earlier and rises a little later. Migrating birds must soon be prepared for another long flight. Many young animals must also be strong enough to endure a long journey.

Now, the soil of the tundra begins to glisten with frost. Birds and animals gather in groups and begin their southward migrations. Only a few birds, including the snowy owl, raven, ptarmigan, and gyrfalcon, remain along with a small number of the larger arctic animals.

Again, open water begins to freeze, and the border between land and sea becomes an unbroken stretch of ice and snow. The bitter cold of the arctic winter will soon spread throughout the roof of the world.

 Arctic Explorers

Explorers first reached the North Pole in 1908 or 1909, depending on whose story is correct. Most history books say that Admiral Robert E. Peary led the first expedition to reach the North Pole. Yet some historians believe that Dr. Frederick A. Cook actually arrived there first.

In April 1909, Dr. Cook sent a cablegram. It read: "Reached North Pole April 21, 1908." A few days later, Commander Peary sent a cable: "I have the Pole, April 6, 1909."

Because the Arctic has such harsh weather conditions, and modern communications did not exist in the early 1900s, reporting on an arctic expedition could take a great deal of time. Regardless of which American explorer arrived first, the North Pole was no longer an unknown place at the top of the earth. For years, explorers from many nations had attempted to find a shortcut from Europe to the Orient. Now, the first step had been taken to make this possible.

The Early Expeditions

Both Admiral Peary and Dr. Cook endured many hardships as they crossed the arctic ice. Since they were pioneers in this cold part of the world, they had to learn much by trial and error.

Both explorers took ships as far as possible along the arctic coast of Greenland. Their ships rammed into the ice and forced their way through it. When the ships could go no farther, the crew unloaded the supplies for the trip and reloaded them onto dogsleds.

In order to keep the sleds as light as possible, they took along only supplies that were most needed. Time, too, was important, and there was little to spare for preparing meals. Men of Dr. Cook's expedition stopped once a day to eat. Then, they often ate raw meat, which they also fed to their dogs. Perhaps the dogs that pulled these sleds deserve part of the credit. Without them, neither Admiral Peary nor Dr. Cook could have reached the North Pole.

On smooth ice, these dogs could travel swiftly. But arctic ice is not smooth. The grinding and cracking of large ice floes cause jagged icy ridges and open lanes of water. In these conditions, fifteen to twenty miles (twenty-four to thirty-two kilometers) per day was a

Admiral Robert E. Peary during one of his arctic expeditions. His chief assistant, Matthew Henson, and four native arctic men were part of the team that reached the North Pole.

good traveling speed for a dog team. Even then, when mountains of ice loomed up ahead and the explorers could not go around them, dogs and men worked together to pull the sleds over these barriers.

North of the tree line in the Arctic, there is nothing to break the force of the wind. No clothing can completely protect a person from these icy blasts. At -76°F (-60°C) in calm weather or in -22°F (-30°C) with a twenty-mile-per-hour wind, exposed flesh can freeze in one minute.

In addition to the extreme cold, the glare created by the sun shining on the snow sometimes blinded the explorers. Often they were sunburned.

Sometimes the men slept in hastily constructed shelters. At other times they slept in snowdrifts. On the arctic ice cap, snow covers both old, solid ice and newly formed ice. At any time, day or night, a sled could break through the ice, sending dogs, people, or supplies into the icy water. Considering the dangers and hardships of traveling in the Arctic, these explorers needed great courage to make such a bold journey.

When the Cook and Peary expeditions reached the North Pole, their journey was only half-finished. They still had to return over the same dangerous route.

Flying to the Pole

Now that explorers with dogsleds had reached the North Pole, other explorers began to think of reaching it in other ways. One of these was an American, Admiral Richard E. Byrd.

Flying was still a new and uncertain way to travel when Admiral Byrd planned his trip by plane to the North Pole. He knew he must fly over 1,600 miles (2,576 kilometers) of polar ice. Byrd learned all he could about airplane engines and oil. The instruments in his tri-motored monoplane, *Josephine Ford*, were the best available.

With fifty men, a sturdy ship, and warm clothing, he started his journey. The expedition's ship sailed to northern Greenland, where the crew set up camp. Then, they prepared the plane to go on.

On May 9, 1926, Admiral Byrd's plane, equipped with landing skiis, was ready. Byrd and his mechanic, Floyd Bennett, brought the plane down a runway built from the top of a hill to the water and took off on their flight.

Almost immediately, they had mechanical problems. When oil started to leak from an engine, they feared that a motor could fail. Since there was no place

to land, the explorers kept going. Next, Byrd dropped an instrument, and it broke. Now, he had only "**dead reckoning**" to determine their location and flight direction. In spite of the crew's problems, the plane reached the North Pole and returned to its base. Byrd and Bennett had made history!

Meanwhile, a Norwegian explorer was also trying to fly over the North Pole. In 1911, Roald Amundsen had led the first expedition to reach the South Pole. Now, three days after Byrd and Bennett, Amundsen passed over the North Pole in a lighter-than-air airship, the dirigible *Norge*. On this trip he crossed the entire Arctic Ocean from Spitsbergen—a group of islands north of Norway—to a point in northern Alaska in North America.

In less than twenty years, four courageous explorers had reached the North Pole and had gained valuable information about the arctic region. Because of these early explorers, people around the world became interested in the Arctic. In the coming years, expeditions of many kinds reached the North Pole, traveling by plane, submarine, and snowmobile. With the help of airdrops of food and equipment, some explorers have even walked to the Pole.

Admiral Richard E. Byrd flew over 1,600 miles (2,576 kilometers) of polar ice to reach the North Pole.

The Steger Expedition

Will Steger, however, headed an expedition that was more like those of Cook and Peary. Rather than rely on mechanical transportation, Steger decided to journey to the North Pole by dogsled. Members of his handpicked team came from the United States, Canada, and New Zealand, and included a woman, Ann Bancroft. After months of survival training in northern Minnesota, eight people and forty-nine sled dogs were ready. On March 8, 1986, the Steger International Polar Expedition set out across the arctic ice from northern Canada.

Because the seven men and one woman would not receive airdrops of food and equipment, they had to carry enough food for the trip to the Pole, and for all the dogs that were needed to haul the added weight. The heavy sleds could not easily cross the huge ridges of arctic ice. Sometimes the team members could travel no more than a few miles a day. Since they had to go around many of these ice barriers, they could not travel in a straight line. They had to travel nearly twice the distance that an airplane would cover flying a direct route to the Pole.

As the voyage wore on, their loads became lighter,

Members of the Steger expedition pull one of their sleds over a pressure ridge on their way to the North Pole.

Will Steger/Firth Photo Bank

and they found less of a need for the heavy sleds. They simply cut off pieces of sleds and burned them for extra warmth in their tent. The expedition had arranged for airlifts to pick up dogs that were no longer needed.

The journey was hard for everyone on the team. Temperatures reached -70°F (-57°C), and when they weren't out pushing with the dogs, they were huddled inside a small tent with no privacy. The tension and close quarters sometimes caused the team members to quarrel.

Outside, the trip wasn't any easier. Crossing ice ridges and **leads** was backbreaking, and often dangerous, work. At one point as Bancroft prepared to jump over an opening in the ice, the edge of the snow gave way beneath her. She fell into the water up to her waist, but grabbed on to the edge and managed to scramble back onto the ice. Bancroft quickly changed out of her wet clothes before they could freeze on her body. She was unhurt, but she said it took two days to get over her chills.

Other members of the expedition were not as lucky. One had been hit by a bouncing sled and injured several ribs. Another suffered from frostbitten feet.

After falling into the cold arctic waters, Ann Bancroft rushes to change her wet, freezing clothes.

The two men had to be airlifted out along with some of the dogs.

Even though there were now only six humans and twenty-one dogs to feed, the supplies were running low. Some of the dogs made matters worse by chewing through their restraining rope and eating twenty precious pounds (nine kilograms) of food.

The team pushed on in a race against the approaching spring thaw and the dwindling food supplies. Finally, they were within twenty miles (thirty-two kilometers) of the Pole, and in good spirits. They traveled along at a fast pace and, at midnight, decided to sleep and check their position in the morning.

On the fifty-sixth day of the expedition, the team awakened to their navigator's announcement: "We don't have to travel today. We're here!" The expedition had unknowingly stopped within two hundred yards of the North Pole. They radioed to verify their position and to call for an airlift out. While they waited for the planes to pick them up, the tired team enjoyed the luxury of crawling back into their sleeping bags.

On May 1, 1986, the Steger International Polar Expedition completed the first confirmed dogsled expedition to the North Pole without resupply. Ann Ban-

Jim Gasparini/Firth Photo Bank

The Steger International Polar Expedition team members hold up the American flag at the North Pole. They also displayed the Canadian flag, and carried the flags of other nations.

croft became the first woman to reach the North Pole. When reporters came to greet the explorers at the Pole, Bancroft read a declaration that expressed the feelings of the whole team: "As we, six adventurers from different parts of the world, stand where the lines of longitude of all countries meet, we believe this journey stands for hope—hope that other seemingly impossible goals can be met by people everywhere."

The Steger team members were not the first to discover in themselves the courage and determination needed to conquer the arctic. And they will not be the last. Yet through their expedition, they joined a select group of history-making arctic explorers.

⑤ *Nautilus 90° North*

Unlike other arctic expeditions, one history-making mission took place beneath the ice. Surrounded by secrecy, the nuclear-powered submarine, *Nautilus*, left its dock in Seattle. The year was 1957, and its U.S. Navy captain was Commander William Anderson. When the underwater trip was underway, Commander Anderson made an important announcement to his crew. The *Nautilus* would travel under the arctic ice and, if possible, to the North Pole.

A Special Submarine and Crew

Excitement mounted. Each member of this hand-picked, highly skilled, and courageous crew worked well as a team. The crew had been through many deep-water missions together. Yet, this one was unlike any journey they had made before.

The whale-shaped *Nautilus* was 320 feet (98 meters) in length—longer than a football field—and 28 feet (8.5 meters) in diameter. The temperature inside

The Nautilus, *a history-making nuclear submarine, heads out to sea.*

the submarine remained a constant 72°F (22°C). Because the vessel did not have to use space to carry batteries and fuel tanks as non-nuclear submarines did, the crew had comfortable quarters.

The *Nautilus* carried all of the latest equipment of its time. It also had several features that had been added for this journey under the ice cap. A specially designed **gyrocompass** had been installed for use near the North Pole, where magnetic compasses are not reliable. In addition, the submarine had upward-pointing **sonar**. This device uses sound waves to locate ice underwater in the same way that ordinary sonar shows the ocean bottom. It would show how thick the ice was as the *Nautilus* moved farther and farther north in the Arctic Ocean. The special sonar would also locate the leads, narrow water passages in pack ice, and the **polynias**, large areas of open water enclosed by ice. The crew needed this information so that the submarine could put up its **periscope**. The *Nautilus* needed refueling only once every two years, and carried enough air to supply the crew for two months.

Even with all its advanced equipment, the vessel's crew had no idea what they would find during their trip into the unknown. Submarines had crept under the edge of the arctic ice before, but none had attempted to go anywhere near the North Pole.

A Test Run under the Ice
Commander Anderson tested the *Nautilus* under these extreme weather conditions in a journey under the ice between Greenland and Spitsbergen. For this trip, he had to rely on instruments. First, he tested the

upward-pointing sonar. The information it provided was charted along with measurements of the distance between the bottom of the submarine and the ocean bottom. For the *Nautilus* to have a safe journey under the ice, it had to receive accurate information from the sonar at all times.

All went well until Commander Anderson attempted to bring the submarine up near the surface to check the area with its periscope. The upward-pointing sonar showed that above them there was an opening in the ice. But as the *Nautilus* ascended, a block of ice smashed the periscope.

Quickly, the *Nautilus* descended, and then made its way out of the ice pack and surfaced. Under difficult conditions, welders repaired the damage.

Commander Anderson was ready to try again. The *Nautilus* traveled deep in the water to within 180 miles (290 kilometers) of the North Pole. Its instruments showed that in some places the ice above the submarine was fifty feet (fifteen meters) thick. Suddenly, an electrical failure caused the gyrocompasses to stop functioning. Without them, it would be too risky to try to complete the journey. Again, Commander Anderson ordered the vessel to turn back.

A crew member checks equipment aboard the Nautilus.

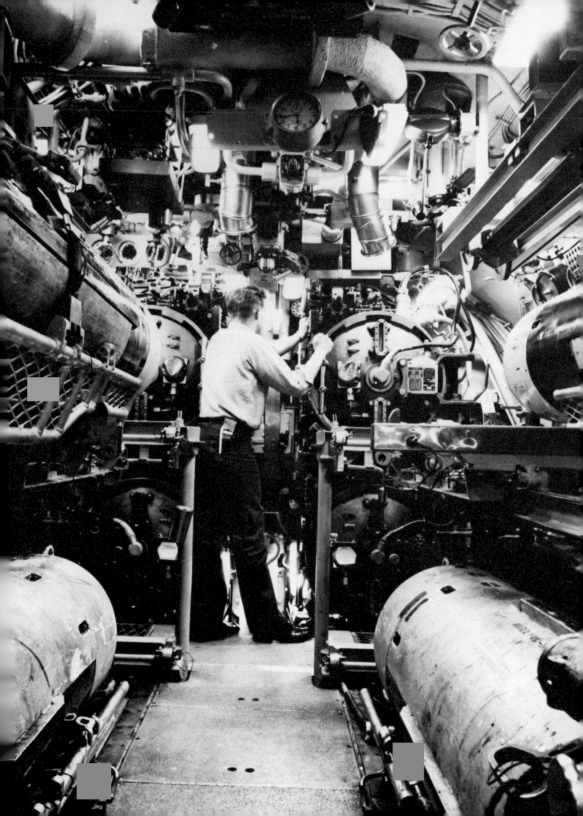

The *Nautilus* reached the safety of the edge of the ice pack. This submarine had gone farther north than any other, but it had not completed its mission. Commander Anderson and the crew wanted the opportunity to try again.

During the next year, Navy workers equipped the *Nautilus* with six new upward-pointing sonar devices. They also installed a closed-circuit television so the crew would be able to look at the underside of the ice.

This time the submarine would attempt to cross the Arctic Ocean from west to east. It crossed the Bering Strait between Alaska and the Soviet Union and moved farther north. Soon the sonar measurements showed that there wasn't much room between the ice above and the ocean floor below. As the *Nautilus* moved farther north, the ice became thicker, but the water did not become deeper. Since the ice above was very irregular, the commander ordered the submarine to slow down and go closer to the ocean floor. This course was risky, but not as risky as hitting a piece of ice overhead. At one spot, the submarine cleared a hanging ridge of ice by only five feet (less than two meters). To the north, the ice would probably become even thicker, and the water shallower.

Commander William Anderson briefs the submarine's crew on ice conditions.

Disappointed, Commander Anderson ordered a course to the south toward open water. Their journey had been started too early in the season.

Nautilus *at the North Pole*

In July 1958, the *Nautilus* made a third attempt at this mission. The submarine submerged beyond Point Barrow, in Alaska, and headed north toward the Pole.

Above the vessel, the ice was still jagged on the underside, but was much thinner than before. The *Nautilus* moved closer and closer to its goal.

Excitement mounted as the crew realized that they would soon reach the North Pole. Commander Anderson stood by in the control room. Finally, he spoke through the intercom: "Stand by. Ten. . .eight. . .six. . . four, three, two, one, mark! August 3, 1958. . . .For the United States and the United States Navy, the North Pole!"

The *Nautilus* had found a passage for nuclear submarines from the Pacific Ocean to the Atlantic Ocean. Its instruments had made an accurate picture of the Arctic Ocean floor and had gathered much valuable new scientific information. Above all, the daring journey had proved that a submarine could travel to the northernmost point on earth.

Their mission accomplished, Commander Anderson set a course to the south. When the *Nautilus* reached a place where it could surface, several hundred miles from the Pole, the submarine's antenna was extended. A radio operator tapped out the message that announced their arrival at the North Pole to the world: *Nautilus* 90° north!

6 Survival in the Arctic

The northern parts of Europe, Asia, and North America extend into the Arctic Ocean. On these continents, a few people pushed northward into the Arctic thousands of years ago. They brought many customs with them from their communities to the south, and adapted their way of life to the arctic region. Today, these people are known around the world as Eskimos. Most arctic people of North America and Greenland call themselves Inuit, which means "human beings." In the far north of Europe and Asia, people call themselves by other names.

Each arctic family or community lived in the way in which the people had the best chance for survival. Families divided the work. Often, men were hunters and trappers, while women prepared and sewed skins and raised dogs. Children helped with chores such as bringing in ice for drinking water. Grandparents and aunts and uncles usually lived with the parents and children.

No matter where they lived, people of the Arctic had much in common. Their greatest enemy was the harsh climate. They survived by adapting to their environment, or surroundings, in every way possible, and by using every available resource. When the people hunted polar bears and seals, they ate the flesh and used the **blubber**, or fat, for fuel. They stretched and dried the animal skins and made them into clothing or tents. Animal bones became human tools.

Arctic Clothes and Houses

Arctic people learned from experience which skins were best suited for clothing. Two layers of caribou skin back to back provided warm winter clothing. Parkas were made so that the people could pull their arms inside for extra warmth. And, if someone fell in the water, they became life preservers. Waterproof sealskin, often padded with fur, made excellent shoe soles. These items of clothing lasted a year, and then had to be replaced.

Arctic people built houses from local materials that suited their needs. Central Canadians, who were nomads, lived in houses made from snow and ice. These igloos worked well for conserving heat, because

This native Alaskan family dresses in both traditional and modern clothes, and travels by dogsled.

their low entrances and domed shape trapped warm air and kept it inside.

Some arctic people, including North Alaskans, built sod houses that were partly underground. They dug a pit, put a support made of driftwood or whalebone across the top, and covered it with sod cut from the tundra and dried. Often, several families shared these earth-sheltered homes.

Nenets, who hunted whales in both the Barents and Kara seas, often lived in tents. The inhabitants of West Greenland made houses of stone and turf.

Arctic Transportation

Transportation in the Arctic varied according to the season. The **umiak**, a kind of boat, often provided water transportation. Its frame was made of driftwood lashed together with sealskin thongs. Stretched seal or walrus hides covered the frame. As a flat-bottomed, lightweight, durable craft, the umiak was well suited to arctic waters. It could survive shocks that would shatter boats made from other materials. More than twenty men could paddle one umiak as they hunted whales.

Some people hunted in **kayaks**, swift little boats

Umiaks like this one are still used by native people in the Arctic.

which were also covered with seal or walrus hides. Hunters lashed their waterproof seal-intestine shirts to their kayaks to keep dry in case of spills.

When arctic people traveled on the snow, many used dogsleds. It took a number of dogs to pull one sled. Certain dogs, such as Alaskan huskies, could survive the harsh climate and could pull the sleds well. Hunters could feed their huskies blubber—the same kind of food they often ate.

Food—a Constant Struggle

Food was a constant problem for everyone who lived in arctic regions. If hunters killed a whale, several families could live all winter from its flesh and blubber. Refrigeration was not a problem. They simply buried the meat in a snowdrift. Whale bones made hunting bows and drying racks for skins.

Most arctic people who lived along the coast hunted seals and walruses for food. They used these animals' skins for clothes, boats, and summer tents. They used the animal fat as oil for lamps to light and heat their homes. **Tendons** of the animals became thread for sewing.

The Lapps lived near the Norwegian Sea where

they received warmth from the Gulf Stream. Because the climate was not as harsh in this area, they were one of the few arctic peoples who were able to do some farming in addition to fishing and whaling.

Reindeer, which are closely related to caribou, were an important resource for many arctic people. Some hunted reindeer by following the migrations of wild herds. Others, like the Lapps, kept herds of reindeer and milked them. In some places they were taught to pull sleds and carry loads. People also rode them. The Evenks, who lived in Siberia near the Yakuts, rode their reindeer high on the shoulders so they would not injure the animals' weak backs.

In the Arctic, people often had to work hard to get water as well as food. Because of the extremely dry air, they needed to drink large amounts of water to replace the water vapor lost in breathing the cold, dry air. Usually, the people had to chop and melt ice to get drinking water. Sometimes, hunters filled the stomach of a freshly killed caribou with snow. The animal's body heat would melt the snow, providing the hunters with water.

Even with all of their **adaptations** to the conditions of the Arctic, life was often a struggle. An unusually

long and severe winter could cause many people to go hungry or even to starve. Parents taught their children what they needed to know to survive—how to hunt, how to keep from freezing in cold weather, how to make animal skins into clothing, and how to water-proof them.

Perhaps the mid-winter darkness was the hardest time of the arctic year. If people had enough food to last through the cold, dark months, they would stay home with their families and visit relatives and friends in the community. Some people used this time to make carvings of animals or humans from ivory or bone. They carved tools such as knives for scraping animal skins, and harpoons for hunting seals. These carvings and tools help us understand what life in the Arctic was like long ago.

As transportation and communication improved, the world learned more and more about the people who lived at the roof of the world. For those who lived in the far north, modern ways of life brought many changes.

Using a handmade drill "powered" by a bow and leather thong device, a native Alaskan carves elegant figures from chunks of bare ivory.

7 The Modern Arctic

During World War II, modern technology came suddenly to the Arctic when air bases were built in some places. Ships and planes brought in equipment and people. Military towns sprang up, bringing thousands of people from the south to areas where just a few hundred arctic people had lived before. After the war, the U.S. and Soviet governments built fighter bases and early warning radar systems in the far north to defend against an attack from the other side of the Pole.

A Changing Way of Life

These new residents bought or traded for many things the arctic people had—from walrus tusks to clothing made from animal skins. At first, the northern people did not understand why these newcomers were so fascinated with items that seemed ordinary to them. Soon, though, the natives offered to sell or trade their belongings. They also became interested in items the people from the south had brought along. Many of these new gadgets, they found, made their way of life easier.

Another big change came about in Alaska. After oil was discovered in the 1960s and 1970s, construction of the Alaskan pipeline began so that the oil could be transported to the south. Almost overnight, heavy equipment and oil workers moved into the areas where the pipeline would be built.

The oil companies needed workers and hired Alaskans at good salaries. Some Alaskan men decided to work on the pipeline for a paycheck and to hunt in the traditional way during their time off. Now, these workers had money to buy all kinds of food, clothing, machines, and household goods. Young people, particularly, were interested in these changes. They were fascinated with snowmobiles and with new kinds of food and clothing. Suddenly, to some of them, the old ways of life did not seem very attractive. They wanted to try all of the new products.

Such rapid changes caused problems in families. Often, parents and grandparents wanted children to follow the traditional ways of life and learn to hunt and fish as their parents and grandparents had. Some-

times, though, the young people in a family decided to try the new ways. They went to schools far away. When they returned, they found that the old ways no longer had meaning for them. Often, there was no place in the Arctic to use what they had learned.

Others decided to continue their traditional ways of life. Yet, even for them, modern technology affected their lives. Because snowmobiles moved faster than dogsleds, some native people acquired snowmobiles. And since rifles made hunting easier, many bought or traded for rifles.

A Blending of Old and New

The old and the new ways were blending. To many people, killing whales seemed less important when they could buy a variety of meats, fruits, and vegetables at a nearby store. Gradually, towns in the Arctic came to have the same kinds of stores as those found throughout the United States. Still, even with all these changes, some of the old ways remain.

Whaling in the Arctic has not changed as much as other types of hunting. Once a whale is killed, many people work together. After pulling it out of the water, they pull away the thick blubber with hooks and di-

Workers build a section of the Alaska pipeline in a mountainous region of the northernmost U.S. state.

Armed with a modern rifle, this native Alaskan hunter waits patiently for a seal to appear. His boat is a traditional one covered by sealskin.

vide the meat in the traditional ways. Then they haul away a slab of blubber, often on a snowmobile. Today, as in the past, the blubber is used for fuel, cooking, and bait for arctic fox traps. As soon as the red meat of this whale is divided, it is taken away and stored in caches dug out of permafrost.

Some Alaskans resent the people from the "south" who have come to their communities in search of new

Native people work together to divide a whale in traditional ways.

sources of natural wealth. They believe this land belongs to the people who have lived here for a long time. Others are pleased by the modern ways. They like the changes in education, medical care, transportation, and communications. And yet, when a job is completed and the company they worked for leaves, they no longer have a paycheck. It is difficult to return to hunting and fishing and go without the money to buy the modern things they have learned to enjoy.

Whether they follow mainly the old or the new ways of life, arctic people must live in two worlds. People from other places will continue to come to the Arctic because governments and industries need new energy sources and are finding them in the far north. As a result, the traditional ways of life will continue to change.

In northern Norway, among the Lapps, less than one person out of ten now follows the reindeer migrations. Many who still herd reindeer use snowmobiles for herding. Since Lapp children go to Norwegian schools, which are often far away, they must live near the school and come home only for visits. In school, the children study the subjects related to modern Norway. At home, they learn how to herd reindeer.

Sometimes these different ways seem far apart. Traditional Lapp parents are upset because their children are not learning more about their heritage. Many young people have left the herds and have become doctors, miners, builders, and teachers. These Lapps have modern homes, automobiles, radios, and television sets.

The 800,000 native people of the Arctic want to have more control over the use of their land and coastal waters. Since they believe it is their right to kill whales for food, they have protested against whaling rules that make it illegal for them to hunt whales. The inhabitants of the far north want to share equally in the development of their homelands. They are meeting with arctic people from other countries to discuss their mutual problems. In some communities, their own candidates have won elections. For everyone, it is a time of great change at the roof of the world.

# The Floor of the World

Just as the Arctic is the roof of the world, Antarctica is the floor. At the South Pole, magnetic compasses spin wildly. Here, the only direction is north.

Seasons in Antarctica are reversed from those of the Arctic. Spring and summer are October through March, and fall and winter are April through September. Like the North Pole, the South Pole has six months of light and six months of darkness.

Antarctica, too, has strange, beautiful lights during its winter months. Here, these southern lights are called the **aurora australis**.

The Coldest Place on Earth

Although the Arctic is known for its extremely low temperatures, Antarctica is the coldest place on earth. This southernmost continent, surrounded by water, is twice the size of the United States. It is shaped somewhat like a circular hump with a narrow point extending to the north—the jagged Antarctic

This map of Antarctica shows the region with the South Pole at its center.

Peninsula, also known as the Palmer Peninsula and as Graham Land. Antarctica has ranges of high mountains and ice plateaus. From its mountain passes, rivers of ice spill into the ocean. The Queen Maud Range divides the continent. One mountain, Mount Erebus, is an active volcano. When it erupts, black ash and fiery lava cover the surrounding ice and snow.

Two seas, the Ross and the Weddell, border Antarctica's northern edge. Each has an ice shelf. The Ross ice barrier is 400 miles (644 kilometers) long, and its jagged cliffs reach 150 feet (46 meters) above the water. Though these two seas pose dangers for ships, they still are the best ocean entrances to the continent at the bottom of the world.

Unlike the Arctic, no warm ocean currents reach Antarctica to temper the climate. And unlike the Arctic Ocean waters, which absorb and give off warmth, the antarctic land mass does not have a similar warming effect. In fact, this region has the coldest temperatures on earth—more than -100°F (-73°C) below zero!

A Land of Extremes

Antarctica has been called "the home of the wind." In its mountainous areas, the howling winds some-

High mountains rise from the ice cap that covers much of Antarctica.

times reach 200 miles (322 kilometers) per hour. They sweep across this continent and whip the seas into huge waves.

Because Antarctica is so cold, it has no rain—**precipitation** comes in the form of snow. The continent receives about four inches (ten centimeters) of moisture each year, which means that it is as dry as a desert. Yet this snow has slowly built up to form the biggest ice cap in the world.

Surrounding Antarctica, the ocean waters remain frozen during the winter months, as in the Arctic. During the antarctic summer, the ice gradually breaks up as it thaws. Waters around Antarctica contain icebergs that have broken off the edges of glaciers as they move slowly downward along mountainsides or valleys and reach the ocean. An iceberg the size of Massachusetts has been seen near the Ross Ice Shelf.

Antarctica has no trees. Some mosses and hardy, slow-growing lichens have adapted to the extreme conditions on parts of this cold continent. Sometimes they grow inside porous rocks of dry antarctic valleys.

Despite its stormy seas, ice cliffs, and ragged, windswept mountains, the Antarctic is a land of great natural beauty. On a sunny day, the blue sea, the

Huge icebergs such as this one break off from the edges of antarctic glaciers.

sparkling white ice and snow, and the clean, fresh air make the extreme cold seem less of a burden to the people who travel there. Fascinating animals—penguins, seals, and whales—thrive in this faraway region. Far more than people, they have adapted to the conditions at the floor of the world.

The Creatures of Antarctica

Antarctica has no large land animals, but penguins, seals, whales, and sea birds live in and above its surrounding waters. Adélie penguins feed on **krill**, small shrimplike creatures, at the surface of the cold antarctic seas. Once in a while, they swim deeper to eat fish and squid.

Antarctic Penguins

The Adélie penguin's streamlined body is well suited to ocean life. In the water, its flipperlike wings serve as paddles. While most birds' bones are hollow, penguins' bones are solid, which gives them added weight for diving. Oily feathers provide the birds with watertight coats. Violent antarctic storms and ocean waves do not bother this creature as it swims in its natural home among icebergs and ice floes. If the water at the surface becomes too rough, it moves to calmer water below the surface.

Though a penguin seldom gets cold in Antarctica,

These Adélie penguins nest in a large colony on the coast of Antarctica.

it sometimes becomes too hot. Then, it must fluff out
its coat to allow some of the heat to escape. In that way
it controls its body temperature.

When a penguin nears the shore, it swims underwater, and then pops onto land like a jack-in-the-box.
While penguins are at home in the ocean, on land these
creatures stand upright and waddle along awkwardly,
or slide on their bellies. To people, they may seem like
little clowns.

Penguins must go to land to nest. In October,
springtime in Antarctica, Adélie penguins land on the
bare rocks where they were hatched. Here, they will
nest in large **rookeries**, or colonies, each pair of penguins in the same nest as the year before. Imagine
trying to locate a certain nest among thousands, crowd-
ed closely together, that look very much alike. Once
the nest is found, the male penguin has to repair it. It
must be scooped out and the sides built up with stones,
replacing those that are missing. The male may have to
go a great distance to find suitable building stones.
While building, he must also keep other penguins from
stealing his stones.

When the nest is completed, the female lays two
bluish white eggs. The male keeps the eggs warm and

guards the nest from **predators** while the female feeds in the ocean for a week or more. To keep the eggs at a constant temperature, the male sits on the nest with the eggs balanced on top of his feet and pressed into his warm body.

When the chicks hatch, they are covered with a feathery down coat. Now, the parents take turns guarding them and waddling to the ocean to get food. After several weeks, because of the chicks' increased appetite, both parents must hunt for food.

With both parents gone, penguin babies face a number of dangers. Blizzards sometimes kill them. Antarctic skuas—hawklike gulls—often swoop down on the rookeries and grab an unprotected chick. Within two months, the remaining penguin babies shed their down, grow adult feathers, and begin swimming in their natural ocean home.

The four-foot (more than one-meter) long Emperor penguin also lives in Antarctica. This large bird may weigh up to eighty pounds (thirty-six kilograms). It raises its young during the coldest part of the year—without building a nest!

The female Emperor penguin lays one green egg. Then the male protects the egg while the female wad-

Emperor penguins raise their young during the coldest part of the antarctic year.

dles to the ocean to feed. If left exposed, the egg would freeze in about one minute.

The male balances the egg on his feet, wraps a fold of skin around it, and stands for two months waiting for it to hatch. To keep themselves and the eggs warmer, many penguins huddle together. During this time, temperatures may drop to -70°F (-57°C), and the birds may have to withstand hurricane-force blizzards. Male Emperor penguins do not eat during these two months. About the time the chick hatches, the mother returns with food and takes over nursery duties while the father goes to the ocean to feed.

Seals and Whales

Several kinds of seals also live in the Antarctic. The Weddell seal is the world's southernmost **mammal**. It reaches ten feet (three meters) in length and 1,000 pounds (454 kilograms) in weight. This seal has a remarkable ability to live on and under the antarctic ice. It feeds underwater and can remain there for forty-five minutes before it must return to the surface to breathe. It keeps breathing holes open by using them constantly and by sawing them open with its front teeth when the holes begin to freeze over.

The Weddell seal has an unusual **metabolism**. Its body burns fuel at more than twice the rate of land animals. Also, a layer of blubber provides excellent protection from the cold. If temperatures become too cold at the water's surface, these seals dive to reach warmer water below. Sometimes they even take naps underwater.

Weddell seal pups are born with fluffy tan fur. If a

A Weddell seal rests on the ice near Scott Base, New Zealand's research station in Antarctica.

pup's coat gets wet, the moisture freezes almost immediately and falls off in ice crystals. That way the pup stays dry. In a warmer area, where the moisture does not freeze so rapidly, the pup might easily become chilled and die.

Of all the antarctic seals, the leopard seal is the most feared predator. This twelve-foot (3.7-meter) long hunter lurks under ice shelves waiting for penguins to swim by. With a sudden burst of speed, it grabs the smaller animal in the water or on the edge of the ice. If a penguin is not available, it may kill another seal. A leopard seal can travel faster on rough ice than a man can run.

Several kinds of whales, including the fin, blue, humpback, and southern right, swim in antarctic waters. The killer whale, which is more closely related to dolphins than whales, also hunts penguins. This creature moves through the ocean near the edge of the ice. While it will chase penguins beneath the water's surface, often the penguins escape by leaping out of the water onto the ice. Of all the creatures of Antarctica, the penguin may be the best adapted to survive in this cold and dangerous environment.

Explorers and Research Stations

In centuries past, a number of explorers set out in search of an unknown "southern land." In 1768, Captain James Cook of England sailed farther south than anyone had sailed before, but did not reach it. Half a century later, a young American, Nathaniel Palmer, sailed his small seal-hunting ship to the long, narrow peninsula that forms the northern part of Antarctica. Twenty years later, an American naval officer, Lieutenant Charles Wilkes, discovered the main part of the continent. The following year, Sir James Clark Ross, heading a British expedition, sailed as far south as the Ross Sea. Then, for nearly a century, the world seemed to lose interest in Antarctica.

In 1911, the Norwegian explorer, Roald Amundsen, decided to try to reach the South Pole. Amundsen planned with great care for a journey by dogsled across the vast, rugged continent. His team members built snow beacons every three miles (five kilometers) to help the expedition find its way back. Every sixty

miles (ninety-seven kilometers), they stored food and other supplies. In an orderly way, but with many hardships, Roald Amundsen and his dogsleds reached the South Pole on December 16, 1911.

Admiral Byrd in Antarctica

After flying to the North Pole in 1926, Admiral Richard E. Byrd organized a larger expedition to explore and study Antarctica and reach the South Pole. In December 1928, two ships, the *City of New York*, and the *Eleanor Bolling*, pulled away from a New Zealand dock. A steel towing rope fastened the two ships together. They sailed toward Antarctica early in the summer, the only time of the year they could get through these iceberg-filled waters. Along the way, these ships were scheduled to meet the Norwegian whaler, *Larsen*, whose captain had volunteered to tow the *City of New York* through the ice pack.

With Admiral Byrd on this expedition were scientific experts in various fields. In all, fifty-three men and 100 sled dogs set out for the southernmost continent.

Admiral Byrd searched for the *Larsen* as huge masses of ice forced the ships to change their course

Roald Amundsen, a famous Norwegian explorer, led the first expedition to reach the South Pole. Amundsen devoted much of his life to polar exploration.

again and again. Time was running out, Finally, they spotted the Norwegian whaler!

Now, the *Bolling* returned to New Zealand for another load of supplies. The *Larsen* towed the *City of New York* through the ice, pushing, pulling, and widening the way. The ice tested the *City of New York*'s ability to withstand its crushing pressure and violent crashes against the ship's timbers. After ten days, they arrived at the open water of the Ross Sea.

When the whaler left, the *City of New York* was on its own. Ahead lay the Ross Ice Shelf. Admiral Byrd had to find a way through this barrier, and locate a place where tons of supplies could be landed—enough to furnish the expedition's members with everything they would need for the winter.

When Byrd found the right place, unloading began at a feverish pace. Nine miles inland, the expedition planned to build a small antarctic town which they had decided to call "Little America." Everybody helped unload supplies, and the dogs pulled load after load to the site where Little America would be built. When the dogs could not pull the loads, men roped themselves to the teams and helped pull. Among the supplies were three airplanes—a single-engine Fairchild, a larger single-engine Fokker, and a huge Ford tri-motor. Byrd planned to use them to help explore the continent. As soon as possible, he made several flights to photograph and map the surrounding region.

In a race against the approaching antarctic winter, the men began to build Little America. They dug foundations in the ice deep enough so that less than half of each building extended above the surface of the ice. Along with their living quarters, they erected radio towers and storehouses.

The *Bolling* returned with another load of supplies. Then, just in time, both ships sailed back to New Zealand for the winter. Soon after they left, ice began to form on the water's surface.

At Little America, the hard work continued. Men hollowed tunnels out of the ice to connect the buildings. They buried the biggest airplane, the *Floyd Bennett*, in a huge hole dug in the ice. At last the expedition was ready for the icy blasts of the antarctic winter.

Late in April, the sun vanished for the winter. Blizzards roared down upon Little America. Temperatures dropped far below zero. In the extreme cold, steel turned brittle, and kerosene became thick.

During the winter, housekeeping chores still had

The Floyd Bennett *in Antarctica before its history-making flight.*

to be done. One of the most difficult jobs was melting enough snow to supply water for the entire "town." Expedition members also gathered scientific data about this icy land. They recorded temperatures, **barometric** and **humidity readings**, and wind speeds.

Meanwhile, Admiral Byrd planned two more expeditions. By October, spring in Antarctica , all was ready. A scientific team, headed by Dr. Lawrence

Gould, started a **geological** exploration of the land masses of Antarctica. As the team's members traveled by dogsled, they dropped off emergency supplies and marked the trail with orange flags on bamboo poles.

Admiral Byrd and his crew prepared to fly to the South Pole in the big Ford tri-motor. Their plane was equipped with skiis that were wider and longer than those ordinarily used on planes. If they had engine trouble and had to land, they could be lost forever in the antarctic wilderness.

Finally, the perfect day came for Admiral Byrd's flight. Five hours after takeoff, the plane's crew saw Dr. Gould's geological party camped at the base of the Queen Maud Range. After dropping a parachute with a few supplies, they were off to the unknown.

Among the mountain peaks, the **altimeter** showed an altitude of 9,600 feet (2,928 meters) above sea level. Now, the *Floyd Bennett* would fly no higher with the weight they carried in the plane. The crew lessened the load by throwing one bag of food overboard. The plane gained some altitude, but not enough to clear the mountains that loomed ahead of them. The crew threw out another and another and still another bag—enough food to last four men for a month.

An artist's view of Admiral Byrd's flight to the South Pole.

With less weight to carry, the *Floyd Bennett* gained enough altitude to fly over the high mountains. Admiral Byrd checked the plane's position again and again. Finally, they reached the South Pole. On that day, November 29, 1929, Admiral Byrd dropped an American flag weighted with a stone as the plane passed over the Pole. Immediately, they turned and flew back toward Little America.

Both expeditions planned by Byrd had been successfully completed during the short spring and summer. Antarctic ground surveys had been made, and the Pole had been reached. Much scientific data had been gathered concerning weather and winds.

The men began to take apart Little America. When the *City of New York* arrived through the ice pack, they were ready to load the ship and start home.

This expedition set the stage for three more expeditions led by Admiral Byrd in the coming years. Each one added to our knowledge of Antarctica. Byrd's daring explorations helped make it possible for research stations to be set up in Antarctica.

International Research Stations

The modern exploration of Antarctica began in 1957 during the International Geophysical Year. Sixty-six nations took part in this event, and twelve nations, including the United States, set up bases in Antarctica. Each base, or station, works independently, but the knowledge gained by its scientists is shared with all of the others. Most scientists do research here only during the antarctic summer months. Some stay throughout the year.

McMurdo Station, known as MacTown, is by far the largest. Here, during the summer, live 800 to 1,200 people—scientists, U.S. Navy personnel, helicopter mechanics, truck drivers, and men and women who keep the town running. They sleep in dormitories and eat in a big mess hall. MacTown has a plant which makes fresh water from seawater, laboratories, a weather station, workshops, an administration building, garages, a chapel, and a gym. Roads link the buildings, and water pipes covered by insulated tin tubes run above ground from building to building. Water is a precious resource. MacTown's residents are allowed two-minute showers twice a week.

Just outside the town is a helicopter pad. Helicopters are an important method of transporation here.

Willie Field, located five miles from town, is the permanent airport for the McMurdo Ice Shelf. It is also a small town with a population of 100 people. Weather reports are transmitted from the field to aircraft every hour. If a special report comes, it usually means bad news about the weather.

On Thanksgiving, MacTown celebrates with a parade. Decorated tractors serve as the floats. The parade is followed by the Penguin Bowl—a football game between the U.S. Navy personnel and civilians of MacTown.

A great deal of research is done at McMurdo Station. Many scientists from McMurdo travel to other field camps, where they live in special tents and collect data for their research projects. **Glaciologists** study the antarctic ice sheet. **Geologists** at this station study Mount Erebus, Antarctica's only active volcano.

Scientists from different fields also share data for common research projects. Because there is very little pollution in the atmosphere over Antarctica, scientists find it is an ideal place to study atmospheric conditions. Researchers are especially interested in the **greenhouse effect**. According to this theory, pollutants trap heat energy in the atmosphere and cause a general warming trend in the earth's climate. Small temperature changes in this cold continent could cause some melting of the ice cap. If large areas of ice melted, the water could raise the ocean level and cause flooding in other parts of the world.

The **ozone hole** is another major research project. The **ozone layer** in the atmosphere screens out much ultraviolet light that is harmful to life on earth. Fluorocarbons, which are used in aerosol sprays, float up to

the ozone layer where ultraviolet rays from the sun break them up and release chlorine **atoms**. The chlorine atoms react with other chemicals in the atmosphere and reduce the concentration of ozone **molecules**, allowing more ultraviolet rays to break through the ozone layer. Between August and October, an "ozone hole"—an area where the ozone layer is very thin—appears in the atmosphere over Antarctica. Although scientists do not know why this "hole" exists, they are using satellites and computerized instruments to get answers. Because the ozone layer is vital to the survival of life on this planet, scientists from many different countries work together to study the changing relationship between humans and the atmosphere.

Two miles from McMurdo is Scott Base, New Zealand's station. Buildings here are connected by sheltered corridors and fire doors. New Zealand scientists conduct research projects at Scott Base, just as scientists from other nations' antarctic stations. The results of such research are shared among all the scientists.

Palmer Station stands on an island just off the Antarctic Peninsula. It lies outside the Antarctic Circle, well north of McMurdo and Scott stations. Here,

A member of a U.S. Navy polar research team uses a drill to test the thickness of an ice floe.

moss grows in deep mounds. Seals nap on the rocky shores, and the sky is full of petrels and skuas. Scientists come to Palmer to carry out research on plant growth, seals, birds, and weather conditions.

Far to the south of Palmer, Scott, and McMurdo stations lies one of the coldest places in Antarctica. Before getting out of the airplane here, visitors must put on a garment that looks like a space suit. Because of the extreme cold, the airplane's engines are not shut down during passenger and cargo unloading or refueling. Visitors must walk slowly so that they will not become dizzy and disoriented at the 9,300-foot (2,837-meter) altitude.

The flags of the nations that maintain antarctic research stations wave noisily in this windy, cold, white land. At the station is a little barber pole with a mirrored globe on top. A sign at the door welcomes visitors to the South Pole Station, also called Amundsen-Scott Station. Living in two-level buildings under an aluminum protective dome, sixteen men and three women stay here for a year at a time. Six of the nineteen are scientists, and each resident has a private room. The South Pole Station has a library, lounge, billiards, showers, modern toilets, and a shop. The

A tunnel connects buildings at the Amundsen-Scott South Pole Station.

food is excellent, which helps during the nine months of the long antarctic winter. Everyone works hard—often seventy hours a week and 365 days a year—and by year's end, they have become a close-knit group.

The South Pole Station is an excellent place to conduct research. Scientists measure ice thickness, **solar radiation**, and the earth's magnetic forces. They also study the way ice surfaces react to traces of gases in the atmosphere. From this station, instruments test the purity of air all over the globe. Other instruments track the movements in the earth caused by earthquakes. Beginning with Admiral Byrd's 1928 expedition, and continuing with today's research stations, our knowledge of Antarctica has greatly increased.

 # Krill, Ice, and Oil

In Antarctica today, airplanes and helicopters transport passengers to the continent from distant airports, or from one antarctic station to another. Icebreaker ships escort cargo ships. Tractors haul supplies across the ice from ships and airfields. Modern, well-equipped research vessels aid scientists.

The Mission of the Hero

The National Science Foundation's research vessel, *Hero*, was built in 1968. For sixteen years it moved busily through the open waters around Antarctica each summer. It glided among icebergs and sometimes slipped within sixty feet (nineteen meters) of leaning ice cliffs, allowing scientists to conduct close-up research. *Hero* was a 760-horsepower **motor sailer**, made of white oak and reinforced at the bow with steel. It was 125 feet (thirty-eight meters) long and had a round bottom which helped it pop up out of the ice. From *Hero*'s deck, scientists studied krill and counted their

For sixteen years the Hero *allowed scientists to conduct close-up research along the shores and among the icebergs of Antarctica.*

eggs. They dived, wearing special dry suits sealed at the neck, to photograph whales.

In 1984, just before the *Hero* was taken out of service, it performed an important rescue mission. An Argentine station, Almirante Brown Base, burned to the ground, leaving seven winter residents stranded in an emergency hut. All other summer ships had left the area. When the *Hero* arrived, seven men, wearing orange survival suits, took one last look at the charred ruins of their winter home, and came aboard. For them, it was a sad sight but a welcome rescue—the last important mission of the *Hero*.

Krill—an Important Resource

Today, scientists are studying krill in the seas around Antarctica, continuing the work they had done aboard the *Hero*. Krill is one of this continent's most important and valuable natural resources. These thumb-length, reddish shrimplike animals are the main food of **baleen whales** and of many other antarctic sea creatures.

Schools of krill circle the continent in areas where warmer ocean water collides with icy antarctic currents. The difference in water temperatures stirs up the ocean and brings to the surface great amounts of **nutrients** from the ocean floor. **Phytoplankton** thrive on these nutrients, and krill feed on the phytoplankton. In this way, krill form a key link in the ocean **food chain**.

A school, or group, of krill may contain tens of thousands of these creatures in a cubic meter of ocean water. Sometimes these schools swim at the water's surface. At other times they swim as far as 600 feet (183 meters) below the surface. Baleen whales cruise through these schools, taking in huge mouthfuls of seawater and krill. These whales then snap their jaws shut and force out the water through their closely spaced **baleen plates**. The krill remains in their mouths, trapped behind the baleen.

Ships from several countries now fish for krill in antarctic waters. The Soviet Union operates 100 giant **trawlers** here. Crews in these vessels bring eight to twelve tons of krill to the surface in one net. They are dried and ground into meal, which is used as food for poultry, farm animals, and farmed fish.

Some scientists believe that krill could be used to help fight world hunger. Krill are the oceans' largest single source of protein, and are rich in vitamins. Hungry people need protein and vitamins. When eaten fresh, krill have very little taste. When frozen or dried, however, they have a strong, unpleasant flavor. **Nutritionists** are looking for ways to improve the taste of frozen or dried krill. Experts say the amount of krill that could be taken from antarctic waters each year would be greater than that of all other kinds of marine life from all the world's oceans.

A Wealth of Fresh Water and Minerals

Ice is another resource of Antarctica. More than two-thirds of the world's fresh water remains frozen in its ice cap. Since some areas of the world lack fresh water for growing crops, watering livestock, and even for drinking, scientists are studying ways to move this frozen fresh water to other places where it is needed. One form in which antarctic ice could be transported is that of an iceberg.

Some scientists think that an iceberg could be towed from Antarctica to southern Australia in two to three months. They estimate that when the iceberg reached Australia, about half of it would be left. This remaining part could be used to supply fresh water and to generate electricity.

Geologists say that Antarctica may have the world's largest coal field. They have also found evidence of valuable deposits of natural gas, iron, copper, gold, and platinum.

The greatest resource of all may be the oil under Antarctica's ice. Geologists have estimated that billions of barrels lie under the ice-covered Weddell and Ross seas. So far, the costs of drilling and transporting antarctic oil are too great to be worth the effort. In

Two scientists climb toward a large snow cliff near Halley Bay in Antarctica.

the future, improved oil-drilling methods and higher oil prices may make this oil more attractive than it is today. Scientists say that offshore oil exploration will not be worth the cost for at least twenty-five years.

Questions about the Future

If much coal, oil, and other minerals are taken from Antarctica, how will such actions affect an environment so fragile that a scar left by a footprint on moss takes ten years to heal? And if large amounts of krill are taken from antarctic waters, will enough remain to feed whales and other antarctic creatures? For the past thirty years, scientists have carried out research that may help government officials protect the world's only unspoiled continent.

In 1959, because of worldwide concern over the use of Antarctica, the Antarctic Treaty was signed by twelve nations—Argentina, Australia, Belgium, Chile, France, Japan, New Zealand, Norway, South Africa, the Soviet Union, the United Kingdom, and the United States. Since then, six other nations have become parties to the treaty, which took effect in 1961. It promotes scientific study and the sharing of information, and bans military activity on the continent. In 1991, when the treaty comes up for review, the participating countries may open certain areas to oil and mineral exploration.

During the 1980s, the Antarctic Treaty nations have attempted to reach agreement on how to control the use of Antarctica's natural resources. The 1980 Convention for the Conservation of Antarctic Marine Living Resources, known as CCAMLR, provides a sys-

The flags of the Antarctic Treaty nations fly at the South Pole Station.

tem to manage antarctic fish and krill. It sets limits on the amounts that can be taken from these waters. In recent years, the treaty nations have been trying to reach an agreement on how to manage the possible development of Antarctica's oil and other mineral resources. So far, they have not been able to agree on a plan, but hope to do so before the treaty is subject to review in 1991. In the meantime, scientists continue to do research in an effort to determine the effects of oil exploration and other activities on the antarctic environment. They will also carry out research in other important areas, such as studying the "ozone hole" in the earth's atmosphere over the South Pole.

Interest in the natural resources of both the Arctic and Antarctica will keep growing as long as nations need energy for homes, factories, automobiles, and other uses. How will the demands of modern life affect the future of the roof and floor of the world? Today's young people—the next generation of government officials and scientists—will help provide the answers.

Appendix A:
Learning More About
the Arctic and Antarctica

The following activities will help you learn more about the Arctic and Antarctica. Choose one or more to begin working on today.

1. Start a scrapbook about glaciers. Include magazine pictures, newspaper clippings, and pictures you draw. What happens to glaciers when temperatures increase? Why do icebergs break off from glaciers? What damage do they do?

2. Read a book about an early arctic or antarctic explorer. Admiral Robert E. Peary, Dr. Frederick A. Cook, or Admiral Richard E. Byrd are excellent subjects. Why do you think explorers were willing to take risks and endure hardships?

3. Find out more about the animals that live year round in the Arctic and Antarctica. How do they endure these harsh conditions? If you visit a zoo, ask how animals such as polar bears adapt to warmer temperatures of the zoo.

4. Draw pictures showing the "old" and "new" ways in the Arctic. Show the differences in food, clothing, housing, and transportation. Draw some pictures that show the old and the new in the same picture.

Appendix B:
Scientific Names for
Arctic and Antarctic Animals

Chapter	Common Name	Scientific Name
3.	American Golden Plover	*Pluvialis dominica*
	Arctic Ground Squirrel	*Citellus parryi*
	Arctic Fox	*Alopex lagopus*
	Arctic Tern	*Sterna paradisaea*
	Brown Lemming	*Lemmus trimucronatus*
	Canada Goose	*Branta canadensis*
	Caribou	*Rangifer caribou*
	Common Loon	*Gavia immer*
	Common Ptarmigan	*Lagopus mutus*
	Gyrfalcon	*Falco rusticolus*
	Musk Ox	*Ovibos moschatus*

Chapter	Common Name	Scientific Name
	Polar Bear	*Ursus maritimus*
	Raven	*Corvus corax*
	Snow Bunting	*Plectrophenax nivalis*
	Snowy Owl	*Nyctea scandiaca*
	Trumpeter Swan	*Cygnus buccinator*
	Wolf	*Canis lupus*
6.	Bowhead Whale	*Balaena mysticetus*
	Ringed Seal	*Phoca hispida*
	Walrus	*Odobenus rosmarus*
7.	Reindeer	*Rangifer tarandus*
9.	Adélie Penguin	*Pygoscelis adeliae*
	Emperor Penguin	*Aptenodytes forsteri*
	Fin Whale	*Balaenoptera physalus*
	Humpback Whale	*Megaptera novaeangliae*

Chapter	Common Name	Scientific Name
	Killer Whale	*Orcinus orca*
	Leopard Seal	*Hydrurga leptonyx*
	Skua	*Catharacta skua*
	Southern Right Whale	*Eubalaena australis*
	Weddell Seal	*Leptonychotes weddelli*
10.	Storm Petrel	*Oceanites oceanicus*
11.	Red Krill	*Euphausia superba*

 *Glossary*

adaptation (add-ap-TAY-shuhn)—the ability of animals (including human beings) and plants to adjust to changes in their environment

altimeter (al-TIHM-uh-tuhr)—an instrument for measuring altitude

Arctic Ocean—the waters surrounding the North Pole between North America and Eurasia

arctic whiteout—the blending of white, low-lying clouds with the snow-covered ground, which makes it impossible to see the horizon

atoms—the small, basic particles of which all substances are made

aurora australis (aw-RAWR-uh aw-STRAY-lihs)—brilliant glowing and moving lights visible in the night sky in the southern polar regions; the southern lights

aurora borealis (aw-RAWR-uh boh-ree-AL-ihs)—brilliant glowing and moving lights visible in the night sky in northern polar regions; the northern lights

baleen plates—a row of stiff material that hangs like teeth on a comb from each side of the upper jaw of a baleen whale; used to trap small plants and animals

baleen whales—whales that have baleen plates rather than teeth

barometric reading—a measurement of pressure of the atmosphere, used in forecasting the weather

blubber—a layer of thick fat between the skin and muscle layers of whales and other marine animals

dead reckoning—used here to mean calculating the position of an aircraft without using navigational instruments

food chain—the connection among living things within a community in nature where larger animals feed upon smaller animals and plants

geological (jee-uh-LAHJ-uh-kuhl)—relating to geology, the study of the history of the earth as recorded in its rocks

geologist (jee-AHL-uh-jist)—a scientist who studies the history of the earth as recorded in its rocks

glacier—a very large mass of ice formed from compacted snow and moving slowly down a slope

glaciologist (glay-see-AHL-uh-jist)—a scientist who studies glaciers

greenhouse effect—a theory which states that artificially and naturally produced pollutants (such as smoke from burning fossil fuels and from volcanic eruptions) increase the carbon dioxide level in the atmosphere; this traps heat energy from infrared rays which causes a general warming trend in the earth's climate

Gulf Stream—a warm ocean current flowing north from the Gulf of Mexico that merges with the North Atlantic Current near Newfoundland

gyrocompass (JY-roh-kuhm-puhs)—an instrument of navigation

hibernation—the state in which animals "sleep" through the winter months, slowing down their metabolism and living off their body fat

horizon—the line along which the earth and sky appear to meet

humidity reading—a measurement of moisture in the air

iceberg—a mass of floating ice which has broken away from a glacier

ice cap—a glacier covering a large area of land and flowing outward from its center

ice floes—sheets of floating ice

kayak (KY-ak)—used here to describe a small one-person hunting boat

krill—tiny, shrimplike creatures which are the main food of baleen whales

lead—used here to mean a narrow passage in pack ice

lichen (LY-kuhn)—a plant that is a combination of algae and fungi

mammal—a warm-blooded animal that nurses its young with milk from the mother's body

metabolism—the sum of the chemical and physical processes by which cells produce the materials and energy necessary for the maintenance of life

migrate—to move from one region to another at certain seasons

molecules—the smallest particles into which a substance can be divided and still have the chemical properties of the original; small groups of atoms

motor sailer—a ship with both a motor and sails

North Pole—the northernmost point of the earth; 90° latitude north

nutrients (NYU-tree-ents)—substances that promote the growth of living things

nutritionist (nyu-TRISH-uh-nist)—a scientist who studies different foods and how the body uses them

ozone hole—an area of the ozone layer where the concentration of ozone molecules is especially thin

ozone layer—a layer of the atmosphere which is made up of ozone molecules; this layer screens out ultraviolet rays that would burn and destroy plants, animals, and people

pack ice—broken, floating ice

periscope—an instrument that can be extended above a submarine to observe conditions above the water

permafrost—permanently frozen subsoil in the arctic and antarctic regions

phytoplankton (fy-toh-PLANK-tuhn)—microscopic plants that drift in the water in great numbers

polynias (poh-LIHN-ee-uhs)—large areas of open water surrounded by ice

precipitation (prih-sihp-uh-TAY-shuhn)—condensed water vapor that falls as rain, hail, or snow

predator (PREHD-uh-tuhr)—an animal that kills and eats another animal

rookery (ROOK-uh-ree)—used here to mean a nesting area for a colony of penguins

rotation—used here to mean the earth's movement or spin on its axis

solar radiation—energy given off by the sun in the form of heat and light (including ultraviolet and infrared light)

sonar—a device for locating objects by means of sound waves

South Pole—the southernmost point of the earth; 90° latitude south

tendon—a cord of tissue that connects a muscle and bone

trawler—a boat with a strong fishing net for dragging along the sea bottom

tundra—the land bordering the arctic ice cap and reaching south to the edge of the northern forests

umiak (OO-mee-ak)—a flat-bottomed, lightweight, durable boat used for hunting in arctic waters

visibility—the distance one can see under certain weather conditions

Selected Bibliography

Bare, Colleen Stanley. *Rabbits and Hares*. New York: Dodd, Mead, 1983.

Beebe, B. F. *American Wolves, Coyotes, and Foxes*. New York: David McKay, 1964.

Begley, Sharon with John Carey and Mary Bruno. "How · Animals Weather Winter." *Newsweek* (February 28, 1983).

Brower, Kenneth. "Two Worlds of the Harp Seal: Above and Beneath the Arctic Ice." *Smithsonian* (July 1979).

Brown, Bruce. "Seal Hunters: Life and Death at the Breathing Hole." *Oceans* (May/June 1981).

Bruemmer, Fred. "The Polar Eskimos: The World's Most Northerly People." *Oceans* (May/June 1981).

——. "Born Again: An Arctic Spring." *Oceans* (July/August 1979).

Dyson, John. *The Hot Arctic*. New York: Little, Brown, 1979.

Eberle, Irmengarde. *Penguins Live Here*. New York: Doubleday, 1974.

Ellis, William S. "Will Oil and Tundra Mix?" *National Geographic* (October 1971).

Greenough, James W. "The Cold War of Little Diomede: An Eskimo Village on the Edge of Today." *Oceans* (May/June 1981).

Hackett, George. "A Trek to the Top of the World." *Newsweek* (May 19, 1986).

Hamner, William M. "Krill—Untapped Bounty From the Sea?" *National Geographic* (May 1984).

Kaplan, James. "Acts of Courage." *Vogue* (March 1987).

Larson, Thor. "Polar Bear: Lonely Nomad of the North." *National Geographic* (April 1971).

McKean, Kevin S. "Mammals of the Sea." *Modern Maturity* (October/November 1984).

Mills, William. "White Lords of the Arctic." *Sea Frontiers* (November/December 1984).

Nicol, Stephen. "Krill Swarms in the Bay of Fundy." *Sea Frontiers* (July/August 1984).

Parfit, Michael. *South Light.* New York: Macmillan, 1985.

Peterson, Roger Tory. "Penguins and Their Neighbors." *National Geographic* (August 1977).

Proctor, Noble S. "Sea Birds of the North: Where Man Cannot Follow." *Oceans* (May/June 1981).

Rahn, Kenneth A. "Who's Polluting the Arctic?" *Natural History* (May 1984).

Ramirez-Heil, Celia. "Antarctica: Life at the End of the Earth." *Americas* (November/December 1981).

Reday, Ladislaw. "The Pull of the Pole: In Search of True North." *Oceans* (January 1985).

Rink, Paul. *Conquering Antarctica: Admiral Richard E. Byrd.* Chicago: Encyclopaedia Britannica Press, 1961.

Steger, Will. "North to the Pole." *National Geographic* (September 1986).

Underwood, Larry S. "Outfoxing the Arctic Cold." *Natural History* (December 1983).

Walsh, James P. "Auguries From Antarctica." *Oceans* (July/August 1982).

Warner, Gale. "Staking Claims on the Last Frontier." *Sierra* (July/August 1984).

Wilsher, Peter and Parin Janmohamed. "Opening the Last Frontier: Managing the Riches of the Polar Regions." *World Press Review* (February 1986).

 Index

 *About the Author*

Alice Gilbreath is the author of more than twenty books for young people during a twenty-five year writing career. She has written four other Ocean World books: *The Continental Shelf: An Underwater Frontier; The Great Barrier Reef: A Treasure in the Sea; River in the Ocean: The Story of the Gulf Stream;* and *Ring of Fire: And the Hawaiian Islands and Iceland.*

Ms. Gilbreath attended Trinity University in San Antonio, the University of Tulsa, and the College of Idaho. She lives in Bartlesville, Oklahoma.